T0027147

HOW TO CONNECT

THICH NHAT HANH

PARALLAX
PRESS

BERKELEY, CALIFORNIA

Parallax Press
2236B Sixth Street
Berkeley, California 94710
parallax.org

Parallax Press is the publishing division of
the Plum Village Community of Engaged Buddhism, Inc.
© 2020 Plum Village Community of Engaged
Buddhism, Inc.
All rights reserved
Printed in Canada

Cover and text design by Debbie Berne
Illustrations by Jason DeAntonis

The material in this book comes from previously published
books and articles by Thich Nhat Hanh.

ISBN:978-1-946764-54-6

Library of Congress Cataloging-in-Publication Data
is available upon request.

6 7 8 9 10 FRIESENS 27 26 25 24 23

CONTENTS

NOTES ON CONNECTING WITH OURSELVES, EACH OTHER, AND NATURE

We are here to awaken from the illusion
of our separateness.

Mindfulness is a healing balm that can put an end to our sense of alienation. It is a nonjudgmental awareness of whatever is happening inside us and around us.

When we bring all our attention to truly connect to whatever we're doing—whether we're walking, breathing, brushing our teeth, or eating a meal—it takes us back to being present in the here and now, which is the foundation of happiness.

When I am mindful, I enjoy everything more, from my first sip of tea to my first step outside. I am here, available to life. And life is available to me.

Practicing mindful breathing and mindful walking, we can connect with the wonders of our body, the wonders of the Earth, and with the whole cosmos.

THE ENERGY OF MINDFULNESS

The energy of mindfulness helps give us the
stability we need to recognize and embrace
our difficult emotions and not let ourselves
be overwhelmed by them. We can be in
touch with the wonders of life around us
and the generosity of Mother Earth, and we
can recognize the many conditions for our
happiness that already exist.

AWARENESS OF BREATHING

In daily life, we often forget that mind and body are connected. Our body is here, but our mind is somewhere else. We easily get caught up in our work, our plans, our anxieties, our dreams, and we aren't living in our body anymore. Today we are living more and more in our mind and becoming increasingly alienated from the natural world. Our breath is the bridge connecting our body and our mind. Returning to our breathing, and following it all the way through from the beginning to the end with awareness, brings body and mind back together, and reminds us of the miracle of the present moment. Awareness of our in-breath and our out-breath calms us down and brings peace back to our body.

SEEING CLEARLY

The practice of harmonizing body and mind
brings clarity, which helps remove wrong
perceptions. When we feel overwhelmed,
confused, or unable to think clearly, we don't
perceive things as they are, and our words and
actions can create suffering and separation
for ourselves and others. When we cultivate
peace inside us, we begin to see things as
they really are. When we're able to see clearly,
understanding and compassion arise, and
anger and jealousy fade away. We accept
ourselves as we are, we accept others as they
are, and we can look at ourselves and others
with the eyes of compassion.

ENJOYING SITTING

Allow yourself to sit quietly, with mindfulness and concentration. Allow your breath to follow its natural rhythm. Enjoy your in-breath and out-breath. Don't strive; relaxation will come. When you are completely relaxed, healing takes place on its own. As we sit, we may become aware that outside, up in the sky, there are so many stars. We may not be able to see them, but they are there nevertheless. We are sitting on an amazingly beautiful planet, which is revolving in our galaxy, the Milky Way, a river with trillions of stars. If we can have this awareness when we sit, what else do we need to sit for? We clearly see the wonders of the universe and our planet Earth. Sitting with this kind of awareness, we can embrace the whole world, from the past to the future, and our happiness is boundless.

COMING HOME TO OURSELVES

In daily life, we are often carried away by our feelings, perceptions, and thoughts. We are seldom free. We're like a leaf floating on the ocean, with the waves tossing us to and fro. We don't have sovereignty over ourselves or our situation. It is so important to be able to come home to ourselves and to cease being the victim of our circumstances. Coming back to ourself with our in-breath and out-breath is the basic practice of peace.

FINDING SOLID GROUND

In our society, countless people suffer from loneliness. We try to cover up our feelings of emptiness by consuming things or by constantly trying to connect with others. Technology supplies us with many devices for staying connected, yet we continue to feel lonely. We might spend the whole day trying to connect—checking email many times, sending texts, posting messages, watching videos—without reducing the amount of loneliness inside. All of us are looking for our solid ground, our true home, a place where we feel safe, comfortable, fulfilled, no longer lonely. But where is home? The Buddha said that home is inside us, that there is a peaceful island within that we can go back to with mindful breathing or mindful walking. You can visualize a beautiful island, with trees, clear streams of water, birds, sunshine, and fresh air. One breath, one step is all we need to feel at home and comfortable in the here and now. When we come back to ourselves like this and take refuge in our inner island, we become a home for ourselves and a refuge for others at the same time.

THE HEART OF PRACTICE

Practicing meditation in our society is very difficult. Everything seems to work in concert to try to take us away from our true self, and we have access to a multitude of things, like the Internet, video games, and music, that help to take us away. Meditation is an opportunity to come back to ourselves, to allow ourselves to take care of our body and our mind, to be aware, to smile, to breathe—not doing anything, just going back to ourselves to see what is going on inside and around us. First we allow ourselves time to release the tension in our body and our mind. Then we can take time to look deeply into ourselves and into the situation we are in.

BRINGING MEDITATION INTO DAILY LIFE

How can we bring meditation out of the meditation hall and into the kitchen and the office? How can we practice in a way that removes the barrier between practice and non-practice? I have a friend who follows her breathing mindfully between phone calls, and it helps her. Another friend does walking meditation between business appointments, walking mindfully between buildings in downtown Denver, and as a result his meetings are often pleasant and successful. We can bring the practice from the meditation hall into our daily lives. Meditation becomes the matter of everyday life.

CONNECTING PAST, PRESENT, AND FUTURE

Mindfulness means to establish yourself in the present moment, but that doesn't mean we can't look into and learn from the past or plan for the future. When we bring past events to the present moment and make them the object of our mindfulness, it teaches us a lot. When we were part of those events, we could not see them as clearly as we do now. With the practice of mindfulness, we have new eyes, and we can learn many things from the past. If you are really grounded in the present moment and the future becomes the object of your mindfulness, you can look deeply at the future to see what you can do in the present moment for such a future to become possible. The best way of taking care of the future is to take care of the present, because the future is made of the present.

TRUE COMMUNICATION

Nowadays we have many means of communication, like smartphones, computers, and television, but communication has become very difficult between partners, father and son, and mother and daughter. Having many electronic devices doesn't necessarily improve the quality of our communication. If we are unable to be in touch with ourselves, to understand ourselves, to know the cause of our suffering, fear, and anger, then we're not in communication with ourselves. If we can't communicate with ourselves, how can we communicate with another person? Coming back to ourselves, we get in touch with our body, feelings, perceptions, and our suffering, and we develop our capacity to listen to ourselves and then to be able to listen to others.

WALKING ON COUNTRY PATHS

I like to walk alone on country paths—rice plants and wild grasses on both sides, putting each foot down on the earth in mindfulness, knowing that I am walking on the wondrous Earth. In such moments, existence becomes a miraculous and mysterious reality.

THE REAL MIRACLE IS TO WALK ON THE EARTH

People usually consider walking on water or in thin air to be a miracle. But I think the real miracle is to walk on the Earth. Every day we are engaged in a miracle, which we don't even recognize: the blue sky, white clouds, green leaves, the curious eyes of a child—our own two eyes. All is a miracle.

MINDFUL WALKING

Walking mindfully is an art. When we are truly present with our steps and our breath, our mind calms and we feel peaceful. In this state we can have many insights; we see things more clearly. Suddenly our problems do not seem so bad, our suffering less intense, and we begin to notice the wonders of life all around us—the beautiful trees and flowers, the sound of the birds.

TOUCHING ONE THING DEEPLY, WE TOUCH EVERYTHING

Standing on the ground in our Plum Village practice center, I am aware that I am standing on French soil. I am also aware that France is linked to the rest of Eurasia. This kind of awareness transforms the spot you are standing on to include the whole Earth. When you practice walking meditation and you realize you are making steps on the beautiful planet Earth, you are liberated from narrow views and boundaries. With each step, you touch the whole Earth, and with this awareness, you liberate yourself from many afflictions and wrong views. When you touch one thing with deep awareness, you touch everything.

INTERBEING

"Interbeing" means that nothing can be by itself alone, but can only inter-be with everything else. Suppose we look at a rose deeply, with mindfulness and concentration. Before long, we will discover that a rose is made of only non-rose elements. What do we see in the rose? We see the cloud, the rain, the sunshine, the soil, the minerals, the gardener. If we were to remove the non-rose elements, there would be no rose left. A rose cannot be by herself alone. A rose has to inter-be with the whole cosmos. We can live our daily life seeing everything in the light of interbeing. Then we will not be caught in our small self. We will see our connection, our joy, and our suffering everywhere.

WE INTER-ARE

When we look at the Earth and at ourselves,
we see that human beings are made only of
non-human elements. Looking into our body,
we see minerals, animals, plants, and other
elements. We can see the whole evolution
of life and of the human species. If we were
to remove the non-human elements, human
beings would disappear. So, to protect
humanity, we must protect the non-human
elements.

THE ONE CONTAINS THE ALL

The present contains the past and the future. When I look deeply into the present, I can touch the past and the future. My ancestors continue in me and are present in every cell of my body. I can be in touch with all my descendants because the future generations are already present in me. Every mindful step made with solidity, peace, and freedom nourishes me, my ancestors in me, and countless generations of descendants waiting to manifest. We practice mindfulness and keep our body and consciousness healthy, not only for ourselves, but for our ancestors, our parents, future generations, society, and the world.

NONSELF

Meditation practice helps us to see the
interconnection and interdependence of
everything that is. There is no phenomenon,
human or otherwise, that can arise on its own
and endure independently. This relies on that;
one thing relies on another in order to arise
and endure. This is the insight of interbeing,
of nonself, which simply means that there
is no separate, permanent entity, including
ourselves; we also inter-are.

LISTENING TO THE BELL

When I was a young monk in Vietnam, each village temple had a big bell, like those in churches in Europe. Whenever the bell was invited to sound, all the villagers would stop what they were doing and pause for a few moments to breathe in and out in mindfulness. At Plum Village, my community in France, we do the same. We have many bells throughout the day—bells in the meditation hall and bells that call us to activities—and every time we hear a bell, we go back to ourselves and enjoy our breathing. When we breathe in, we say, silently, "Listen, listen," and when we breathe out, we say, "This wonderful sound brings me back to my true home." Our true home is in the present moment.

STOPPING FOR A RED LIGHT

When we see a red light or stop sign, we can
smile and say thank you, because it's helping
us reconnect with ourselves and the present
moment. The red light is a bell of mindfulness.
We may have thought it was preventing us
from reaching our destination more quickly.
But now we know the red light is our friend,
helping us to resist rushing and calling us
to return to the present moment, where we
can meet with life and peace. The next time
you are caught in traffic, don't fight. If you sit
back and smile to yourself, you will enjoy the
present moment and make everyone in the car
relaxed and happy.

BELLS OF MINDFULNESS

Over time, we can identify our own "bells of mindfulness"—a sound or a repeated daily action that reminds us to return to our conscious breathing. It might be a stop sign, the first three rings of the telephone, climbing up or down a flight of stairs, opening and closing the door, or walking up the path to your front door at home. You can also download a bell of mindfulness to sound on your computer at work. We can use all of these as opportunities to remind ourselves to pause and come back to our body and to the present moment.

RETURNING TO YOUR HERMITAGE

One sunny morning following a rainstorm, I decided to spend the day in the woods near my hermitage. Before setting out, I opened all the windows and doors, so the sun could dry things out. But in the afternoon, the weather changed. The wind blew, and dark clouds gathered. Remembering I had left everything open, I returned home right away. When I arrived, my hermitage was in a terrible condition. It was cold and dark inside, and my papers were scattered all over the floor. First, I closed all the windows and doors. Then I lit a lamp and made a fire in the fireplace. And finally, I picked up the papers from the floor, put them on the table, and weighted them down with a stone.

Now there was light and warmth. I sat by the fire and listened to the wind. I was aware of my in-breath and out-breath and I felt very content. There are moments in our daily life when we feel miserable, empty, and cold, and it seems everything is going wrong. We think, "This is not my day." That's exactly how my hermitage was that day. The best thing to do at such times is to go back to yourself, to your island within, to your hermitage, close the windows and doors, light a lamp, and make a fire. This means you have come to a stop and are no longer busy running around, thinking, or talking. You've gone back to yourself, back to your hermitage, and become one with your breathing.

OUR HERMITAGE IS WITHIN

Each of us has a hermitage to go to inside—a place to take refuge in and breathe. This doesn't mean we're cutting ourselves off from the world. It means we're getting more in touch with ourselves. Breathing is a good way of doing this. We begin by noticing our in-breath and out-breath. With the in-breath, we can say, "Breathing in, I am in the present moment," and with the out-breath, "Breathing out, this is a wonderful moment." As we repeat this, we can simply use the words "present moment" for the in-breath, and "wonderful moment" for the out-breath. Breathing mindfully will make our hermitage a lot more comfortable. When our hermitage inside is comfortable and peaceful, then our contact with the world outside of us will become more pleasant.

THE TELEPHONE

Our phone is such a convenient means of
communication. It saves us travel time and
expense and it connects us with each other.
But our phone can also tyrannize us. If we
spend time on our phone without awareness,
we waste precious time and energy; we lose
ourselves, and we can't accomplish much.
Many of us are victims of our own phone.

When your phone rings, you can practice
mindful breathing and come back to yourself
before answering. Remember, you are your
own master. Say to yourself:

Breathing in, I calm my body.
Breathing out, I smile.

Before making a call or text, we can practice mindful breathing and recite this verse:

> Words can travel thousands of miles.
> May my words create mutual
>   understanding and love.
> May they be as beautiful as gems,
> as lovely as flowers.

There are many ways to bring happiness to others right in this moment. We can start with speaking kindly. The way we speak to others can offer them self-confidence, hope, and trust. Mindful speaking is a deep practice. When we choose our words carefully, we can make people happy.

LISTENING TO OURSELVES

Mindfulness of listening and speaking can help us restore communication. We begin by coming home to ourselves and practicing mere recognition, which means listening to whatever thoughts and emotions rise up without judging them, and then letting them pass without holding on to them. We can learn to listen to our own suffering. We don't have to try to get away from ourselves or cover up unpleasant or uncomfortable feelings. We are there for ourselves, to understand ourselves, our suffering and our difficulties, and to transform. Before we can listen to another person, we need to spend time listening to ourselves.

HAPPINESS AND SUFFERING INTER-ARE

To enjoy happiness doesn't mean we have no suffering. The main affliction of modern civilization is that we don't know how to handle the suffering inside, so we try to cover it up with all sorts of consumption, and the marketplace is full of items to help distract us. Until we're able to face our suffering, we can't be available to life, and happiness will continue to elude us. The art of happiness is also the art of suffering well. When we learn to acknowledge, embrace, and understand our suffering, we suffer much less. One of the most difficult things for us to accept is that there is no place where there is only happiness and no suffering. If we focus exclusively on pursuing happiness, we may see suffering as only getting in the way of our happiness. The practice of mindfulness, our capacity to dwell in the present moment, is the best way to be with our suffering without being overwhelmed by it. With awareness of our in-breath and out-breath, we generate the energy of mindfulness, and take care of our suffering by recognizing, accepting, and embracing it tenderly. With mindfulness, we're no longer afraid of pain; and we can generate the energy of understanding and compassion that heals and brings happiness both to ourselves and to others.

ALLEVIATING WORRY

Some of us have a habit of worrying, even though we know it isn't helpful. When we worry, we're not able to be in touch with the wonders of life or be happy. We might feel we'd like to get rid of our worry. But worry is part of us. So, when worry comes up, we have to know how to handle it—peacefully, nonviolently, with tenderness. We can say "Hello my little worry, I know you are there. I hear you and I will take good care of you." With the energy of mindfulness, we recognize and embrace our worry, our agitation, our fear, and our anger, tenderly, just as we would hold and calm a crying baby who is sad, angry, or afraid.

DON'T BE FOOLED

The feeling of loneliness is universal. There is often little real communication between ourselves and others, even within the family, and our feeling of loneliness sometimes pushes us to engage in sexual relationships. We believe this will make us feel less lonely, but that is a false belief. We shouldn't let ourselves be fooled. When there is not enough communication with another person at the level of the heart and spirit, a sexual relationship will make both people suffer and will widen the gap between them. In the end, we will feel even more lonely.

RECOGNIZING AND TRANSFORMING ATTACHMENT

All of us have a tendency to become attached. When we're born, attachment to self is already there. Even in wholesome love relationships, there's some possessiveness and attachment, but if it's excessive, both people suffer. If a father thinks he "owns" his son, or if one person in a relationship controls the other, love becomes a prison and the flow of life is obstructed. Without mindfulness, attachment becomes aversion. Both attachment and aversion lead to suffering. Look deeply to see the nature of your love and the degree of attachment. Then you can begin untangling the knots. The seeds of true love are already there inside us. By looking deeply, the seeds of suffering and attachment shrink, the positive seeds grow, and we arrive at a love that's spacious and all-encompassing.

LISTENING TO OUR
INNER CHILD

We all have a wounded child inside us who
needs to be listened to. If we are mindful,
we will hear the child's voice calling for help.
Go back and tenderly embrace the wounded
child. You can talk directly to the child with the
language of love: "In the past, I left you alone.
I'm very sorry. I know you suffer. I neglected
you. Now, I am here for you. I will do my best to
take good care of you." You can cry with your
wounded child. Whenever you need to, you
can sit and breathe with the child. "Breathing
in, I am here for you. Breathing out, I will take
good care of you." Talk to your child several
times a day, and healing will take place.
Embrace your inner child tenderly, reassure
the child that you'll never let them down or
leave them alone again. The wounded child

has been left alone for so long. Listen carefully to your inner child. When you climb a beautiful mountain or contemplate the sunset, invite your child within to enjoy it with you. Touching the present deeply, you can heal the past.

Our wounded child may represent several generations. Our parents and ancestors may not have known how to care for their wounded child, and so they may have transmitted that child to us. Our practice is to end this cycle. Healing our wounded child, we liberate ourselves, and we help liberate the one who hurt or abused us. We may begin to see that those who hurt us were themselves victims of abuse who had not transformed their own suffering. Practicing with our inner child lessens our suffering and brings transformation.

LISTENING TO OTHERS

The most effective way to show compassion to
another person is to listen to them. Once we
know how to listen to our own suffering with
compassion, we can listen to someone else
with the same compassion, and our listening
is like a salve for their wounds. We listen with
only one purpose, which is to give them the
chance to speak out what is in their heart and
to suffer less. We refrain from interrupting or
attempting to correct what we hear. When
we see and understand the other person's
suffering, compassion is born in our heart, and
we no longer blame them for their behavior.
We only want to help and bring relief. We can
do this by listening deeply, with compassion,
and without judgment.

LISTENING WITH ATTENTION

Whenever I talk with a friend, I listen with all my attention to their words and tone of voice. As a result, I hear their worries, dreams, and hopes. It isn't easy to listen so deeply that you understand everything the other person is trying to tell you, but every one of us can cultivate this capacity.

UNTYING INTERNAL KNOTS

Some of us cannot think about our father or mother without feeling anger or sadness. The suffering we experience as children accumulates and forms blocks of pain, anger, and frustration in our consciousness that tie us up and obstruct our freedom. These internal knots have the power to drive us and dictate our behavior. Each of us has internal formations like this that we need to take care of. With the practice of meditation, you can undo the knots and habitual behaviors that bind you. You experience transformation and healing for yourself and for your strained or broken relationships. In this way, you won't pass on your suffering to the next generation.

RECONCILIATION BY TELEPHONE

In the retreats we offer, on the fourth day, everyone is urged to apply what they've learned to restore communication with someone. Many of us are estranged from a family member; perhaps you're angry with your father and can't think of anything kind to say to him. Now you've practiced for a few days, looking into your own suffering and the suffering of the other person. If they are in the retreat, it's much easier, because they've heard the same teachings and have been practicing too. But if they are at home, you can use your mobile phone to call them. Practice mindful breathing and walking so you are calm. After three or four days of practice, there's been a transformation in you, and when you dial the number and hear their voice, suddenly you find you're capable of listening deeply and using the language of loving kindness. "Dad, I know you have suffered a lot for many years, and yet I was unable to help you. I only made the situation worse. I've been stubborn and angry because I didn't understand your difficulties. It was not my intention to make you suffer. Please tell me about yourself, about your suffering and difficulties." When you speak like this, the heart of the other person will open, communication will be restored, and there will be healing for both of you. The seed of compassion and the capacity to listen deeply are in your heart; you just need mindfulness to touch them. Reconciliation is possible in any relationship, even between conflicting parties or nations.

RECONCILIATION TAKES
PLACE WITHIN

Once someone wrote to me, saying, "I have
made mistakes in the past. Now I would like
to reconcile with my daughter. But every
time I write and ask her to meet with me, she
refuses. What can I do?" You may believe that
reconciliation is only possible by meeting with
the other person. But actually, reconciliation
takes place inside us. Accepting responsibility
for our actions is the first step. When you can
accept your unskillfulness and shortcomings,
compassion and insight are born in your heart.
If you have not achieved reconciliation within
yourself, it will be difficult to reconcile with
the other person. With internal reconciliation,
peace and love become possible. When you
embody peace and love, you can change the
situation more easily.

THE FOUR MANTRAS

The four mantras are magic formulas that can be practiced in daily life to help us connect with others, especially our loved ones. A mantra has the power to transform the situation—but it only works if we are really present and available for the other person.

The first mantra is "I am here for you." The greatest gift we can give to others is our true presence. This establishes real connection.

The second mantra is, "I know you are there, and I am very happy." To be truly present and know that the other is also there is a miracle. When you are really there, you are able to recognize and appreciate the presence of the other—the full moon, the magnolia flowers, or the person you love.

The third mantra is, "Darling, I know you suffer." When you are mindful, you notice when the person you love suffers. Your presence alone will relieve a lot of their suffering.

The fourth mantra is the most difficult. It is practiced when you yourself are suffering and you believe the other person is the one who has caused your suffering: "I am suffering. Please help." Many people cannot say this because of the pride in their heart. In true love, there is no place for pride. Hearing your words, the other person will come back to themselves and look deeply. Then the two of you will be able to sort things out, let go of wrong perceptions, and reconcile.

THE INSIGHT OF NO SELF

Sometimes when I practice calligraphy, I invite my mother, my father, or my ancestors to draw with me. Although they have already passed away, we are drawing together; I touch the insight of no self, and it becomes a deep practice of meditation. The meditation, work, joy, and life become one. When I walk, I walk for my father. I walk for my mother. I walk for my teacher. I walk for my students. Maybe your mother or father never knew how to walk mindfully, enjoying every moment and every step. So we can walk in mindfulness for them and all of us will benefit.

TWO HANDS OF ONE BODY

One day, I was trying to hang a picture on the wall. My left hand held a nail and my right hand a hammer. I was not very mindful, and instead of pounding the nail, I pounded one of my fingers. The right hand immediately put down the hammer and took care of the left hand as though she was taking care of herself. My right hand considers the suffering of my left hand as her own suffering. My left hand didn't say, "Right hand, give me that hammer. I want justice!" There's an inherent wisdom in my left hand, the wisdom of nondiscrimination. When we have this kind of wisdom, we don't suffer. My left hand never fights my right hand. Both hands enjoy harmony and understanding.

MORNING WALK

Every morning when I wake up and get dressed, I leave my hut and take a walk. Usually the sky is still dark, and I walk gently, aware of nature all around me and the fading stars. One morning, after walking, I came back to my hut and wrote: "I am in love with Mother Earth." I was as excited as a young man who has fallen in love. When I think of the Earth, I think, "I'm going to go out into nature, enjoying everything beautiful, enjoying all its wonders," and my heart is filled with joy. The Earth gives me so much. I'm so in love with her. It's a wonderful love; there's no betrayal. We entrust our heart to the Earth and she entrusts herself to us, with her whole being.

MAKING AN ALTAR

On the altar in my hermitage in France there
are images of Buddha and Jesus, and every
time I light incense, I am in touch with both
of them as my spiritual ancestors. When you
touch someone who authentically represents
a tradition, you touch not only their tradition,
you also touch your own. You may like to
make your own altar on a bookcase or table,
perhaps with fresh flowers, pebbles, or something beautiful you have found in nature. You
may like to include a photo or two of family
members who have passed away to keep their
presence alive in your life. In Vietnam and
other East Asian countries, every home has
a family altar. Whenever there is an important
event in the family, like the birth of a baby or a
child going off to college, we offer incense and

announce the news to our ancestors. When we return home after a long trip, the first thing we do is offer incense to our ancestors and announce that we are home. A home altar is a way to stay connected to nature, to our ancestors, and to our spiritual lineage, to pay respect to them and keep them alive within us.

EACH SECOND IS A JEWEL

Every second has in itself many jewels, and each minute, each second, is itself a jewel. When we look into the jewel of this very second, we see the sky, the earth, the trees, the hills, the river, and the ocean—so beautiful! Let us profit deeply from each moment that is given us to live.

OUR CONNECTION WITH THE EARTH

The Earth purifies and refreshes. Whatever we throw on the Earth—fragrant flowers, urine, or excrement, the Earth doesn't discriminate. She accepts everything, whether pure or impure, and transforms it, no matter how long it takes. We humans have done many careless things that have harmed the Earth, and yet she does not punish us. She brings us to life, and she welcomes us back to her when we die. When we look deeply and feel this connection to the Earth, we begin to feel admiration, love, and respect. When we understand that the Earth is so much more than simply the environment, we are moved to protect her as we would protect ourselves. She is us, and we are her. With this kind of communion, we no longer feel alienated.

THE SUN MY HEART

The heart in my body is not my only heart. The sun in the sky is also my heart. If my own heart failed, I would die instantly. If the sun stopped shining, the flow of life would stop and I would also die. The sun is our heart outside our body. It gives all life on Earth the light and warmth necessary for existence. Plants live, thanks to the sun. Thanks to the plants, we and other animals can live. All of us—people, animals, plants, and minerals—get nourishment from the sun, directly and indirectly. Seeing this, we easily transcend the duality of self and nonself and see that the environment is us.

HAPPINESS IS NOT AN
INDIVIDUAL MATTER

I know of a young boy who was about eleven
or twelve years old. The day before his birthday, his father asked him, "What would you like
for your birthday? I'll buy you whatever you
want." But the boy was not at all excited. He
knew his father could afford to buy him anything, but he didn't want any more things. He
was unhappy because his father was always
so busy and rarely spent time at home. After a
few moments, the young man said, "Dad, what
I want is you!" What children want the most
is the presence of the people they love. If his
father could only understand this, no doubt he
would practice mindful breathing or walking
for a few minutes, lay aside all his projects, and
make himself available for his son. No one is a
separate independent self. Father and son are

not entirely separate realities. The father exists in the son, and the son exists in the father. The son is the continuation of the father into the future, and the father is the continuation of the son back to the source. If the son is not happy, the father cannot be happy, and if the father is not happy, there is no way the son can be happy. Their happiness is deeply connected. Happiness is not an individual matter.

DO I UNDERSTAND YOU WELL ENOUGH?

Loving speech and deep listening are wonderful methods for opening the door of communication with loved ones, including children. As parents, we should not use the language of authority, but the language of love and understanding with our children. Only then will they confide in us their difficulties, suffering, anxieties, and dreams, which will help us to understand them better and love them more. If our love isn't based on understanding, our children won't experience it as love. You can sit next to your child, or even your partner or a friend, and ask, "Do you think I understand you well enough—your difficulties, your suffering, your dreams and deepest desires? Please tell me. I don't want to make you suffer. If I don't yet understand, then please help me to understand."

THE WISDOM OF NONDISCRIMINATION

One time a young person asked me, "Why do we give different names to different things, since they're really together, they're really one?" This is a very good question. I replied that names are at the root of so many problems. We give places different names, like North America, Iran, and Iraq. But in fact, they all belong to the Earth. Israel and Palestine are two hands of the same body. You have to work for the survival of the other side if you want to survive yourself. Survival means the survival of humankind as a whole, not just a part of it. Only when we can touch the wisdom of nondiscrimination can we all survive.

EATING IN MINDFULNESS

Whenever we eat in mindfulness, we connect more deeply with our planet. Getting in touch with the Earth is what will heal our suffering, our depression, our sickness. When we eat a piece of bread mindfully, we see the Earth, the sun, the clouds, the rain, and the stars in our bread. Without these elements, the bread wouldn't exist. We see that the entire cosmos has come together in this one piece of bread to nourish us.

DRINKING TEA

Drinking tea is a wonderful way to set aside
time to communicate with yourself. When
I drink my tea, I just drink my tea. I stop all
my thinking and focus my attention on the
tea. There is only the tea. There is only me.
Between me and the tea there is a connection.
I breathe in, and I am aware that my in-breath
is there, I am aware that my body is there, and
I am aware that the tea is there. It's wonderful
to have the time to drink your tea, to be there,
body and mind together, established in the
here and the now. When you are truly present,
you become real, and the tea becomes real.

PRAYER

Perhaps all prayer comes back to our simple human desire for happiness and feeling connected both to other people and to something greater than ourselves. Prayer, whether silent, chanted, or in meditation, is a way to return to ourselves in the present moment and touch the peace that is there. It is, simultaneously, a way to put us in touch with the universal and the timeless. Our true happiness comes from being fully conscious in the present moment, aware of our connection to everything else in the universe.

TRUE CONNECTION

Every time you walk even a short distance,
whether from your home to the bus stop, or
from the parking lot to your workplace, you
can choose to walk in a way that every step
brings you joy, peace, and happiness. Walking
like this, we feel connected to ourselves, to
the earth under our feet, and to everyone and
everything around us. It's not because you
have a telephone that you feel connected.
I've never had a cell phone, yet I've never felt
disconnected from anyone. What connects
us is our mindful breath and mindful steps. If
you want to connect with others, all you need
to do is to practice walking meditation every
morning after breakfast on your way to work.
Walking in peace and freedom, we become
connected to all of life.

COLLECTIVE PRACTICE

Meditation is no longer the work of individuals;
meditation in our time should be a collective
practice. The whole country, the whole world,
can meditate together and look deeply at
the real questions of poverty, exclusion,
and despair.

TAKING ROOT

Leaves are usually looked upon as the children of the tree. Yes, they are children of the tree, born from the tree, but they are also mothers of the tree. The leaves nourish the tree by combining raw sap, water, and minerals with sunshine and carbon dioxide. In this way, the leaves become the mother of the tree. We are all children of society, but we are also mothers; we have to nourish society. If we are uprooted or disconnected from society, we cannot transform it into a more livable place for ourselves and our children. Meditation is not an escape from society. It is a practice that can help us become more firmly rooted in society, so that the leaf can nourish the tree.

PRACTICING FOR OURSELVES AND EACH OTHER

An individual is made of non-individual elements. The kind of suffering that you carry in your heart, that is society itself. When you meditate, you bring society with you, you bring all of us with you. You meditate not just for yourself, but for the whole society. You seek solutions to your difficulties not only for yourself, but for all of us.

A COMMUNITY OF PRACTICE

When we practice with others, there is
mutual support, and the practice becomes
easy. In Buddhism, a practice community is
called a *sangha.* We can make our family
into a sangha. If everyone learned the art of
deep listening and loving speech, we could
make our workplace, our neighborhood,
our local government, and even Congress
into a community of practice. Being part of
a sangha can heal feelings of isolation and
separation. We practice mindfulness together,
sit together, walk together, sometimes we
may drink tea, garden, or eat side by side and
wash dishes together. Just by going about
our daily activities with fellow practitioners,
we can experience a tangible feeling of love
and acceptance. The sangha is a garden, full

of many varieties of trees and flowers. When we can see ourselves and others as beautiful, unique trees and flowers, we can truly grow to understand and love one another. One flower may bloom in early spring, and another in late summer. One tree may bear many fruits and another tree may offer refreshing shade. No one plant is greater than another.

COMMUNITY IS EVERYWHERE

We can start to build a sangha with our partner, our family, our household, or we can meet with friends once a week or once a month to practice together. We practice to realize peace, happiness, and joy in that small sangha. At the same time, we see our small sangha in the context of the larger sangha; we are practicing with the help of our teachers, parents, friends, and all living beings in the animal, plant, and mineral worlds. Live your daily life so you feel their presence with you all the time. Do whatever you can to bring happiness and well-being to the air, the water, the rocks, the trees, the birds, and the humans.

TODAY'S DAY

Life is found only in the present moment.
I think we should have a holiday to celebrate
this fact. We have holidays for so many important occasions—Christmas, the New Year,
Mother's Day, Father's Day, even Earth Day—
why not celebrate a day when we can live
happily in the present moment all day long?
I would like to declare today "Today's Day," a
day dedicated to touching the Earth, touching
the sky, touching the trees, and touching the
peace that is available in the present moment.

COLLECTIVE INTELLIGENCE

When ants are all together in an anthill, there is intelligence, there is cooperation, there is thinking and insight; they know exactly what to do and what not to do. The anthill behaves as an organism. If five, ten, or a dozen ants are placed away from the rest, they don't know what to do; they get confused and run around aimlessly. What the community of ants does, no individual ant can do. There is no leader in the community of ants; the same is true of bees and termites. When individuals come together as a sangha and the sangha begins to operate as an organism, there is intelligence, imagination, insight, stability, and wisdom.

AN ORCHESTRA WITHOUT A CONDUCTOR

In our brain, a multitude of neurons are communicating with each other, interacting to produce thoughts, feelings, and ideas, but no one neuron is the director; it's like an orchestra without a conductor, or a beehive with all the bees working together. The queen bee isn't the leader; her only duty is to produce the next generation of bees. Looking into our body, we see a multitude of cells working together, but there's no boss. A sangha, a community of people practicing mindfulness, concentration, and insight together, is like a beehive with everyone working together in harmony.

EVERYONE NEEDS A SANGHA

In 1966, I was exiled while in the West to call
for peace for my country. I felt like a bee on
a mission, cut off from the hive, like a cell
outside of the body, at risk of drying up and
dying. As a practitioner, when you are cut off
from your sangha, this is also a kind of death.
I didn't want to let this happen to me, so I
contacted people in the academic community
and spiritual leaders from various traditions
who were working for peace, and together we
created a community of practice. I knew that
without a sangha I couldn't survive. Wherever
I go, I always carry my sangha with me in my
heart, and wherever I am, I always begin to
build a sangha.

TEA MEDITATION

In Plum Village, we often have tea meditation. We take time to prepare everything beforehand so that we can enjoy a quiet and peaceful atmosphere. We arrange cushions and mats in a circle, and prepare a beautiful vase of flowers in the center. Then we come together to enjoy a cup of tea, a cookie, and the company of others for about an hour and a half. We have nothing to do and nowhere to go. In the serene, intimate, and informal atmosphere, we share poems, songs, and stories. Usually, it only takes a few minutes to drink a cup of tea, but in taking time to be truly present for one another like this, we nourish mutual understanding and happiness.

PEACE IN ONESELF,
PEACE IN THE WORLD

With mindfulness, the practice of peace, we can begin to transform the wars in ourselves. There are techniques for doing this. Conscious breathing is one. Every time we feel upset, we can stop what we're doing, refrain from saying anything, and breathe in and out several times, aware of each in-breath and each out-breath. If we're still upset, we can go for a walk, mindful of each slow step and each breath we take. By cultivating peace within, we bring about peace in society. It depends on us. To practice peace in ourselves is to minimize the number of wars between this and that feeling, or this and that perception, and we can then have real peace with others as well.

DAILY MINDFULNESS IS THE BASIS OF CHANGE

It is the daily practice of mindfulness that will bring about real emancipation and social change. Social action must be based in real, solid mindfulness practice. Political and social change will be much easier when we have a foundation of spiritual practice. With a regular practice of mindfulness, we'll have a clear direction and know which actions to take and which not to take—in our daily life, and in helping our communities to engage in social change. Our communities have a deep desire for social justice. This can be obtained only through the transformation of our collective consciousness. All political actions, from protests to lobbying campaigns, will be meaningful only when they are born of our freedom, our understanding and compassion, and our peace and joy.

OLIVE TREES

One year I went to Italy for a retreat and I
noticed that the olive trees were growing in
small groups. I was surprised and asked why
they'd been planted in groups of three or four.
Our friends explained that each group was
actually just one tree. One winter had been
so harsh that all the olive trees died. But deep
down the roots were still alive, and when
spring came, young shoots sprouted in groups,
so that instead of having one trunk, each
tree had three or four. They appeared to be
separate olive trees, but in fact they were one.

TRUE COMMUNITY

Is it possible to make Congress or Parliament into a community? Our society is based on the dualistic view of self and other, a view which furthers self-interest. We aren't used to thinking of ourselves as a community or perceiving reality in terms of universal harmony and peace. Coming back to ourselves and looking deeply into the situation of our society, we can recognize the factors that have brought disharmony, conflict, and suffering. At the same time, we recognize that there is a path of mindfulness and harmony that can bring about transformation and healing, that will lead to true brotherhood and sisterhood, true connection, and true community.

GLOBAL COMMUNITY

Whatever people may feel about it, humankind will become a global community. Separation and destruction are taking place all over the world. Can we be like the ants and the bees and work together in harmony? Community building is an art. A community of practice is an organism which functions according to the principles of mindfulness, concentration, and insight. In order to avoid discord, destruction, and suffering, each of us can bring our practice of mindfulness, our insights, and experience of community building to help create this global community.

RESTORING BALANCE

The Earth has already experienced a lot
of suffering in the past from which she has
managed to recover. She has experienced
natural disasters such as collisions with other
planets, meteorites, and asteroids, as well
as severe periods of drought, forest fires,
and earthquakes. Yet she has been able to
restore herself after all these events. Now we
are putting so much strain on the Earth by
polluting the atmosphere, warming the planet,
and poisoning the oceans, that she can't heal
on her own. The Earth has lost her equilibrium.
We have lost our connection with the Earth
and her natural rhythms. All of us have to
accept responsibility for what is happening
to the Earth, see our role in this process, and
know what to do to protect Mother Earth.

We can't just rely on her to take care of us; we also need to take care of her. Unless we restore the Earth's balance, we will continue to cause destruction, and it will be difficult for life on Earth to continue. We need to realize that the conditions that will help to restore the necessary balance come from inside us, from our own mindfulness, our own level of awareness. Our own awakened consciousness is what can heal the Earth.

FRESH HERBS

During the Vietnam War, we had so many things to worry about—bombs falling every day and people continuing to die. My mind was focused only on how to help stop the war, the killing, and the suffering. I didn't have time to get in touch with the wonders of life that are refreshing and healing. My body and mind weren't getting the nourishment I needed. One day, one of my students brought a basket of fresh herbs to go with our lunch—in Vietnam, we normally have fresh herbs at every meal—and I just marveled at them. I realized that I hadn't had the time to think of things like fresh herbs, the simple, everyday things that represent the wonders of life.

This experience taught me I shouldn't immerse myself so completely in work that I get drowned in it. I should have time to live, to get in touch with the refreshing and healing elements that are in me and around me.

A simple plate of fresh herbs was enough to restore my balance. Those of us who are activists always want to succeed in our attempt to help the world, but if we don't maintain a balance between our work and our spiritual nourishment—our practice of mindfulness—we can't go very far. The practice of walking meditation, mindful breathing, getting in touch with the refreshing and healing elements in and around us is crucial for our survival, and will help us be able to continue our work for a long time.

A GLOBAL ETHIC

The world in which we live is globalized.
Economies halfway around the world affect
our own. Our politics, education, culture,
and consumption extend beyond national
boundaries. Our ethics, our human values,
also need to be globalized. A new global order
calls for a new global ethic that everyone
can embrace. A shared code of ethics is the
key to addressing the true challenges of our
time. Around the world, we are facing climate
change, violence, and wars. Fanaticism,
discrimination, division, injustice, economic
crises, and the destruction of the environment
affect us all. We can sit down together, as
people of many nations and traditions, to
identify the causes of global suffering and to
find solutions. If we look deeply with clarity,

calm, and peace, we can see the causes of our suffering and find a way out. We are many different cultures and nations, each with its own values, ways of behaving, and criteria for ethical conduct. Every country, every culture and tradition can offer something beautiful. It will take all our collective wisdom to make a global code of ethics. With insight from all the world's people and traditions, we can create a global ethic that is based on mutual respect.

CREATING REAL CHANGE

There is a revolution that needs to happen, and it starts from inside each one of us. When we change the way we see the world, when we realize that we and the Earth are one, and when we begin to live with mindfulness, our own suffering will start to ease. When we're no longer overwhelmed by our own suffering, we will have the compassion and understanding to treat the Earth with love and respect. Restoring balance in ourselves, we can begin the work of restoring balance to the Earth. There is no difference between concern for the planet and concern for ourselves and our own well-being. There is no difference between healing the planet and healing ourselves. Real change will happen only when we fall in love with our planet. Only love can show us how to live in harmony with nature and with each other and save us from the devastating effects of environmental destruction and climate change. When we recognize the virtues and talents of the Earth, we feel connected to her and love is born in our hearts. We want to be connected. That is the meaning of love: to be at one. When you love someone, you want to take care of that person as you would take care of yourself. When we love like this, it's reciprocal. We will do anything for the benefit of the Earth and we can trust that she, in turn, will do everything in her power for our well-being.

THE EARTH FROM SPACE

In 1969, for the first time ever, people saw images of the Earth taken by astronauts orbiting the moon. This was the first time we could see the totality of our planet. Seen from space, we could see the Earth as one living system. We could see how beautiful, but also how fragile the Earth is, and her atmosphere too—just a tiny thin layer protecting us all. To the astronauts, the Earth appeared as a dynamic, living, and constantly glowing jewel. When I first saw those pictures, I was amazed. I thought, "Dear Earth, I didn't know that you were so beautiful. I see you in me. I see myself in you."

COLLECTIVE AWAKENING

Many of us all over the world are trying to bring about a kind of collective awakening. If we manage this, all will be well, and we will know how to live together in harmony with each other and with the Earth. Together we will know what to do to save the planet and make a future possible for our children and their children. This change of consciousness can be achieved when we realize the interdependent nature of reality, a realization that each of us can experience in a unique way. This realization is not the result of any ideology or system of thought; it is the fruit of our direct experience of reality in its multiple relationships.

SHARING OUR INSIGHT

We must learn to speak out so that our voices
and the voices of all our spiritual ancestors
can be heard in this dangerous and pivotal
moment in history. We should offer our light to
the world, so it will not sink into total darkness.
Everyone has the seed of awakening and
insight within their heart. Let us help each
other touch these seeds so that everyone
will have the courage to speak out. We have
the tools. We have the path. We have the
ability, with practice, to have the necessary
insight. We only need to begin. With one
step, with one breath, we can commit to living
our daily lives in a way that brings happiness
and well-being to the planet, to our beloved
communities, and to ourselves.

PRACTICES FOR CONNECTING

———

Practices to help us reunify body and
mind and get back in touch with life
in the present moment.

COMING HOME TO THE BODY

It is good to have a regular practice of sitting meditation, even if it's just ten minutes before bed or in the morning before beginning the day. You can also practice sitting meditation on the bus, in the car while waiting at a red light, at the airport, and at work before a meeting or during a break. Maintaining a regular practice is the way to establish and maintain a connection with our body, feelings, and mind. This brings us peace and clarity. When you sit down, make sure you are in a comfortable position with your back straight but not rigid, eyes closed or half open, jaw relaxed, and shoulders relaxed. A half-smile on our lips helps us relax all the muscles in the face and gives rise to a feeling of peace and joy. We start by bringing our awareness to our breathing and following it, noticing the gentle rising and falling of our abdomen. We relax the whole body and release all the tension. It's very simple and enjoyable. Meditation is not hard labor! You can repeat these phrases silently as you sit, or you can lie on the ground to practice deep relaxation of the body, going through each part and releasing tension, generating a feeling of well-being.

I breathe in and follow my in-breath the whole way through, from the beginning to the end.
I breathe out and follow my out-breath the whole way through, from the beginning to the end.

Aware of the gentle movement of air going into my body, I breathe in.
Releasing any tension I may be holding in my body, I breathe out.

In touch with my shoulders and abdomen,
   I breathe in.
Relaxing my shoulders and abdomen,
   I breathe out.

Aware of the state of my body, I breathe in.
Feeling grateful to my body, I breathe out.

I breathe in and dwell peacefully in the
   present moment.
I breathe out and know this is a
   wonderful moment.

GUIDED MEDITATION

Mindfulness has two functions. The first is to get in touch with the wonderful and beautiful things all around us. The second is to get in touch with the difficult emotions, like anger, fear, pain, and sorrow inside and around us. Mindfulness can help us recognize and embrace these difficult feelings and transform them. We can practice guided sitting meditations to help us in this practice of recognizing and transforming difficult emotions or negative thinking. We always begin with cultivating awareness of the breath and the body—calming the breath and the body, relaxing and releasing tensions in the body. Then we can move on to identifying and embracing our thoughts and feelings. Here is a simple guided meditation for you to practice:

Breathing in, I am aware of my in-breath,
Breathing out, I'm aware of my out-breath.
In, out.

Breathing in, my breath becomes deep,
Breathing out, my breath becomes slow.
Deep, slow.

Aware of my body, I breathe in,
Relaxing my body, I breathe out.
Aware of body, relaxing body.

Aware of my feelings, I breathe in,
Calming my feelings, I breathe out.
Aware of feelings, calming feelings.

Aware of my thoughts, I breathe in,
Gladdening my thoughts, I breathe out.
Aware of thoughts, gladdening thoughts.

Breathing in, I feel happy to be alive,
Breathing out, I smile to life.
Happy, smiling.

WALKING MEDITATION

When we walk with mindfulness, our feet connect with Mother Earth. We walk with gentle steps and bring our full awareness to each step. Steps like these have the power to rescue us from the state of alienation and bring us back to a place of true refuge, reconnecting us with ourselves and with the Earth. Every step can be nourishing and healing.

Wherever we walk, whether at the airport, in the supermarket, or on a forest path, we're walking on Mother Earth. Walk in a natural, relaxed way, matching your steps to your breath. As you breathe in, you may take one, two, or three steps. As you breathe out, you may want to take a few more steps than you did with your in-breath. For example, you might take two steps as you breathe in, and three steps as you breathe out.

In, in.
Out, out, out.

You may also like to try slow walking meditation. We take one step with each in-breath and one step with each out-breath. We walk for ourselves, our loved ones, and the whole world. We walk mindfully, gathering nourishment from the Earth, and with each step we can vow to protect all living beings. Instead of counting, we can also use words to accompany our steps.

Coming home to the Earth.
Returning to my source.

Taking refuge in Mother Earth.
Releasing all my suffering to the Earth.

Mother Earth is in me.
I am in Mother Earth.

HEALING THE WOUNDED CHILD

As children, we were very vulnerable. We got hurt easily. This pain is still inside us. The wounded five-year-old child in us is still there and needs to be heard. If we want to be able to connect with others and understand them, we have to be able to do the same for ourselves first. We can practice getting in touch with our inner child, to recognize, embrace, and transform their pain. We can practice reflecting on ourselves as a five-year-old, and then we can do the same for our parents, our siblings, or those who we think have made us suffer. Here is a simple guided meditation for you to practice:

Breathing in, I follow my in-breath.
Breathing out, I follow my out-breath.

Breathing in, I calm my body.
Breathing out, I smile to my body and relax.

Breathing in, I see myself as a five-
    year-old child.
Breathing out, I smile to the five-year-old
    child in me.

Seeing how innocent, vulnerable and fragile
    I was at the age of five, I breathe in.
Comforting my five-year-old self, I breathe out.

Feeling the suffering and loneliness of myself at
    the age of five, I breathe in.
Soothing and embracing my five-year-old,
    I breathe out.

Recognizing my five-year-old's strong emotions,
    I breathe in.
Calming my five-year-old's strong emotions,
    I breathe out.

Feeling love and compassion for myself at the
age of five, I breathe in.
Accepting myself as I am, I breathe out.

Now do the same meditation for your mother,
father, or other person who you think has hurt
you in the past. Not only will you feel more
connection to them, but love, understanding,
and compassion will be born in your heart.

Breathing in, I see my mother as a five-year-
old child.
Breathing out, I see how innocent, fragile, and
vulnerable she was at the age of five.

(and so on . . .)

LOVE MEDITATION

Sending love and compassion to ourselves and others has the power to heal and transform our suffering. We can send our healing energy of love and compassion first to ourselves, then to those we love, then to someone we have difficulties with, and finally to all beings everywhere who are suffering. We can say "May I," then "May you," "May they," and finally "May all beings." You might like to recite this every evening before bed, or during your daily meditation practice. Like this we can connect with the whole world, with all beings everywhere.

> May I be peaceful, happy, and light in
>   body and mind.
> May I be safe and free from injury.
> May I be free from anger, fear, and anxiety.

May I learn to look at myself with the eyes
of understanding and love.
May I be able to recognize and touch the seeds
of joy and happiness in myself.
May I learn to identify and see the sources of
anger, craving, and delusion in myself.

May I know how to nourish the seeds of joy
in myself every day.
May I be able to live fresh, solid, and free.
May I be free from attachment and aversion,
but not be indifferent.

123

CONSCIOUS BREATHING, A PEACEFUL REFUGE

Our breathing is a stable, solid ground in which we can take refuge. No matter what is going on inside us, our breathing is always with us, like a faithful friend. Whenever we're carried away by our thinking, when we're overwhelmed by strong emotions, or when our mind is restless and dispersed, we can return to our breathing. We bring our body and mind together and we collect, calm, and anchor our mind. We're aware of the air coming in and going out of our body. With awareness of our breathing, it naturally becomes light, calm, and peaceful. At any time of the day or night, whether we're walking, driving, working in the garden, or sitting at our desk, we can return to the peaceful refuge of our own breath.

OTHER TITLES IN THE SERIES

How to Eat

How to Fight

How to Love

How to Relax

How to See

How to Sit

How to Walk

RELATED TITLES BY THICH NHAT HANH

Be Free Where You Are

Being Peace

Calming the Fearful Mind

Love Letter to the Earth

The Miracle of Mindfulness

No Mud No Lotus

Present Moment Wonderful Moment

Reconciliation

The World We Have

Monastics and visitors practice the art of mindful living in the tradition of Thich Nhat Hanh at our mindfulness practice centers around the world. To reach any of these communities, or for information about how individuals, couples, and families can join in a retreat, please contact:

Plum Village
33580 Dieulivol, France
plumvillage.org

Magnolia Grove Monastery
Batesville, MS 38606, USA
magnoliagrovemonastery.org

Blue Cliff Monastery
Pine Bush, NY 12566, USA
bluecliffmonastery.org

Deer Park Monastery
Escondido, CA 92026, USA
deerparkmonastery.org

**European Institute of
Applied Buddhism**
D-51545 Waldbröl, Germany
eiab.eu

Thailand Plum Village
Nakhon Ratchasima
30130 Thailand
thaiplumvillage.org

Healing Spring Monastery
77510 Verdelot,
France
healingspringmonastery.org

Maison de l'Inspir
77510 Villeneuve-sur-Bellot
France
maisondelinspir.org

**Asian Institute of
Applied Buddhism**
Ngong Ping, Lantau Island
Hong Kong
pvfhk.org

**Nhap Luu-Stream
Entering Monastery**
Porcupine Ridge, Victoria 3461
Australia
nhapluu.org

Mountain Spring Monastery
Bilpin, Victoria 2758
Australia
mountainspringmonastery.org

The Mindfulness Bell, a journal of the art of mindful living in the tradition of Thich Nhat Hanh, is published two times a year by our community. To subscribe or to see the worldwide directory of sanghas (local mindfulness groups), visit **mindfulnessbell.org**.

THICH NHAT HANH FOUNDATION

planting seeds of Compassion

works to continue the mindful teachings and practice of Zen Master Thich Nhat Hanh, in order to foster peace and transform suffering in all people, animals, plants, and Our planet. Through donations to the Foundation, thousands of generous supporters ensure the continuation of Plum Village practice centers and monastics around the world, bring transformative practices to those who otherwise would not be able to access them, support local mindfulness initiatives, and bring humanitarian relief to communities in crisis in Vietnam.

By becoming a supporter, you join many others who want to learn and share these life-changing practices of mindfulness, loving speech, deep listening, and compassion for oneself, each other, and the planet.

For more information on how you can help support mindfulness around the world, or to subscribe to the Foundation's monthly newsletter with teachings, news, and global retreats, visit **tnhf.org**.

**PARALLAX
PRESS**

Parallax Press, a nonprofit publisher founded by Zen
Master Thich Nhat Hanh, publishes books and media
on the art of mindful living and Engaged Buddhism. We
are committed to offering teachings that help transform
suffering and injustice. Our aspiration is to contribute
to collective insight and awakening, bringing about
a more joyful, healthy, and compassionate society.

View our entire library at **parallax.org**.